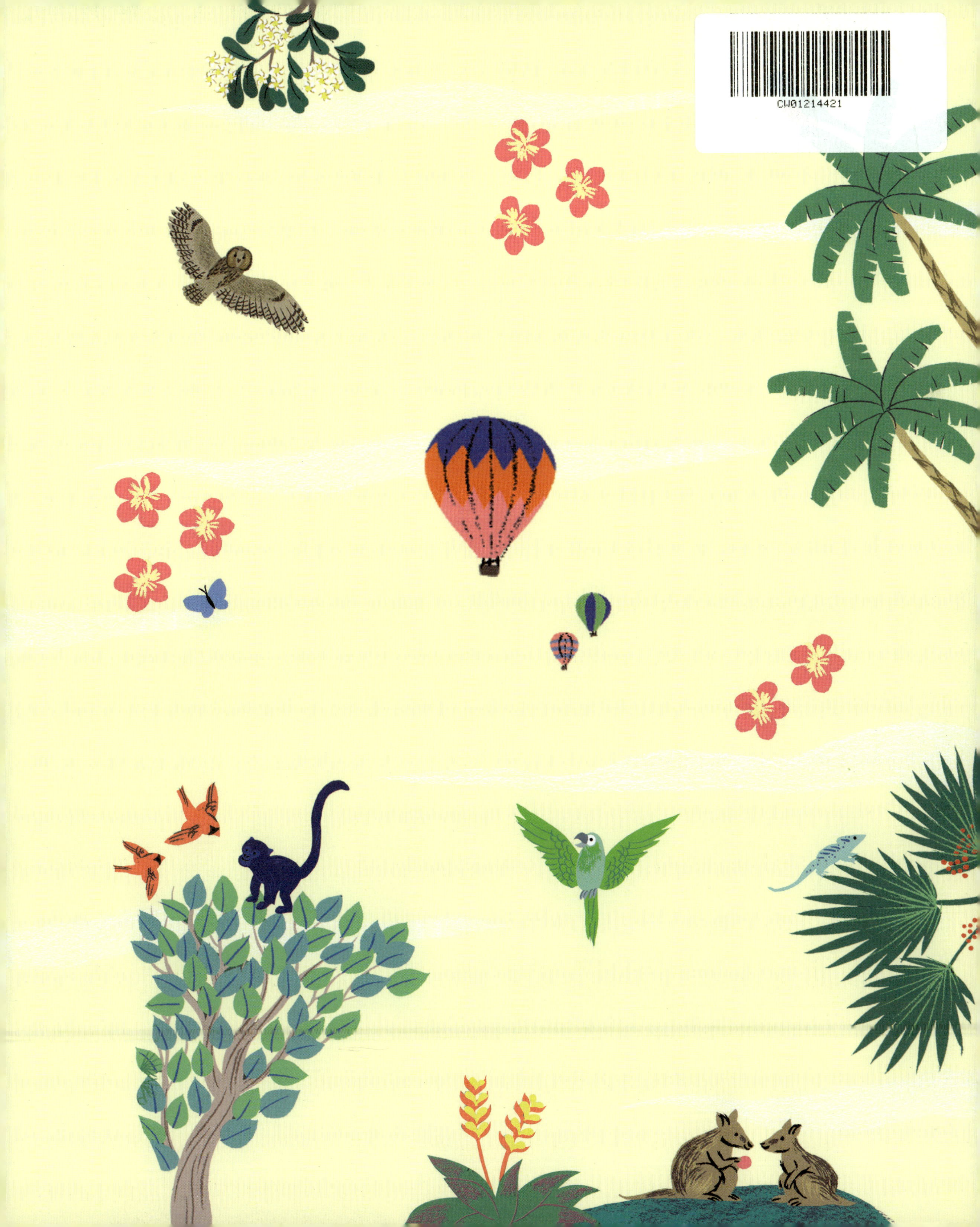

For Apolline and Agathe
— E. M.

DK | Penguin Random House

Editorial Abi Luscombe, Rea Pikula
Design Nidhi Mehra, Dheeraj Arora, Eleanor Bates
Consultants Dr. Molly Rosenbaum, Dr. Nick Crumpton
Managing Editor Laura Gilbert
Senior Production Editors Robert Dunn, Nikoleta Parasaki
Production Controller Magdalena Bojko
Publishing Manager Francesca Young

First published in 2019 in French
as *Ma Cabane Du Bout Du Monde*.

This edition published in Great Britain in 2022
by Dorling Kindersley Limited
DK, One Embassy Gardens, 8 Viaduct Gardens, London, SW11 7BW

The authorised representative in the EEA is Dorling Kindersley Verlag
GmbH. Arnulfstr. 124, 80636 Munich, Germany

Text and illustrations copyright © L'Agrume 2019, 2022
Layout and design copyright © 2022 Dorling Kindersley Limited
A Penguin Random House Company
10 9 8 7 6 5 4 3 2 1
001–327001–Apr/2022

All rights reserved.
No part of this publication may be reproduced, stored in or introduced into a retrieval system, or transmitted, in any form, or by any means (electronic, mechanical, photocopying, recording, or otherwise), without the prior written permission of the copyright owner.

A CIP catalogue record for this book
is available from the British Library.
ISBN: 978-0-2415-3842-5

Printed and bound in China

For the curious
www.dk.com

MIX
Paper from
responsible sources
FSC™ C018179

This book was made with Forest Stewardship Council™ certified paper – one small step in DK's commitment to a sustainable future. For more information go to www.dk.com/our-green-pledge

My Perfect Cabin

Written by Emmanuelle Mardesson
Illustrated by Sarah Loulendo

DK

Hi there! I'm Lucile, and I am on a search for the perfect cabin. I'm not sure what it should look like or what materials it's built from.

I'm going on a journey round the world to see where all my friends live, so I can pick up a few ideas about different types of cabins. Will you come along?

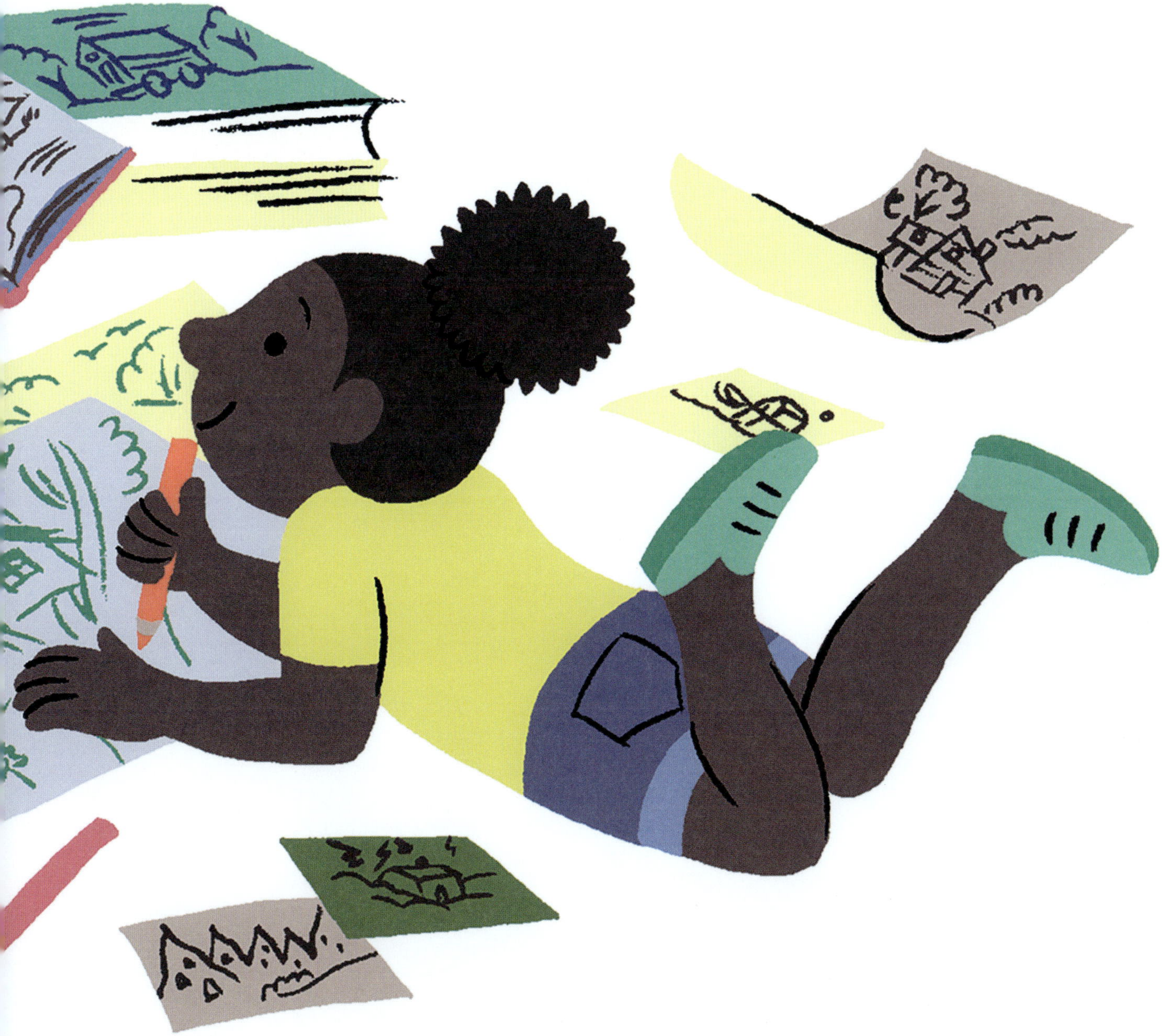

The first cabin on my journey belongs to my friend Erik. I was walking through the trees when I suddenly spotted it sticking out from under a layer of grass, as if it grew from the forest floor. It has three wooden walls and the fourth side is buried in the earth. People often pass by without even noticing it is there, which makes it the perfect hideaway. The only giveaway is the smoke from the chimney when Erik uses the fireplace to cook and bake. His baking is very popular with his friendly neighbours, the elk, the badger, and the little, feathered wagtail. We make Erik's delightful soft, fluffy cardamom buns together, and the smell brings all of his neighbours to the window.

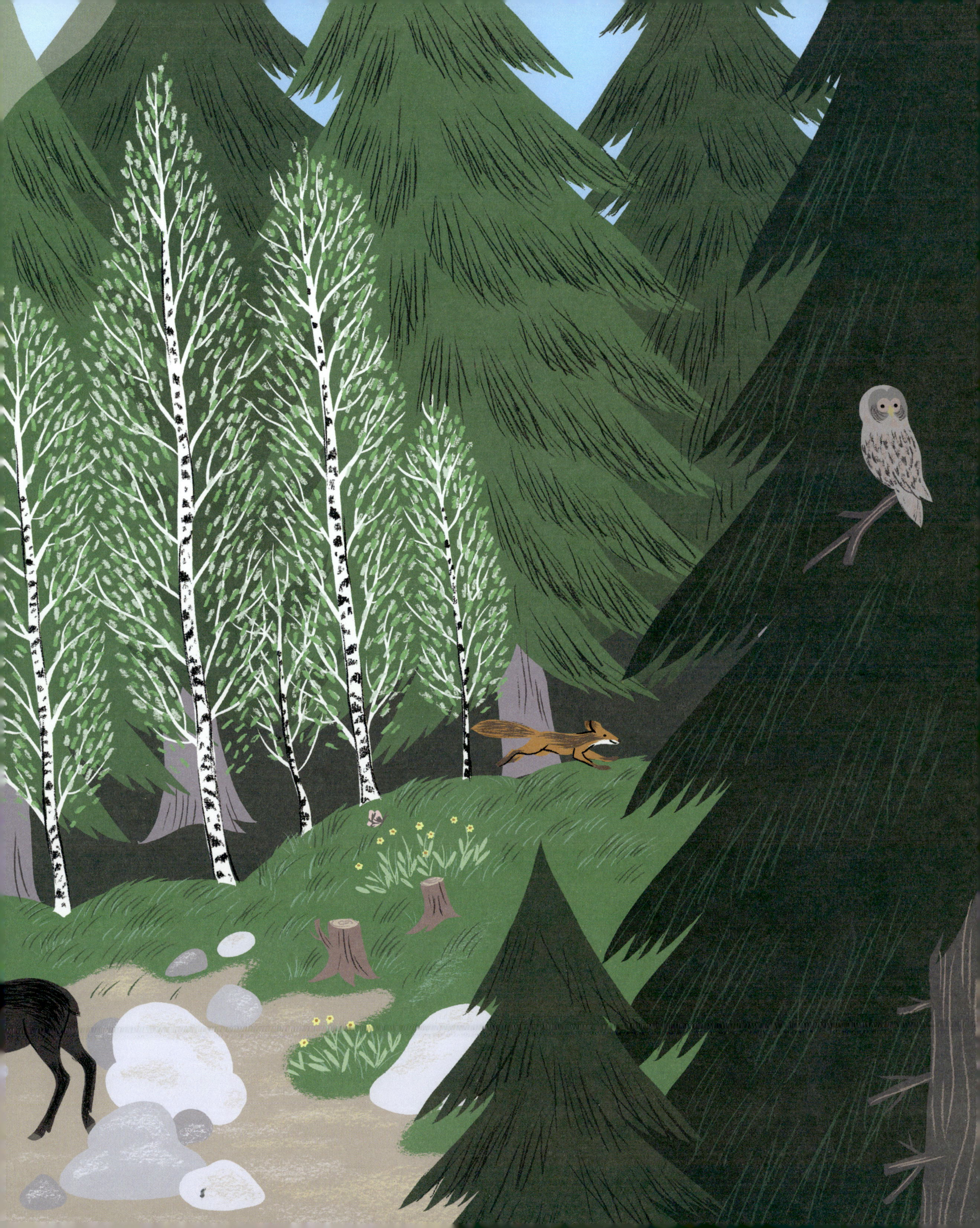

Anna's cabin is high up in the sky, so I had to climb a rope ladder to reach it. There is a whole tree growing in the middle of her living room! Her home is nestled in a rainforest, surrounded by buzzing, chirruping, ribbiting wildlife. Anna loves playing her guitar to entertain the animals. I sit back and listen while, all around me, little monkeys beat their hands to the music, the trees rustle to the rhythm, and the toucans toot delightfully. Anna's mint-green parrot squawks along noisily, too!

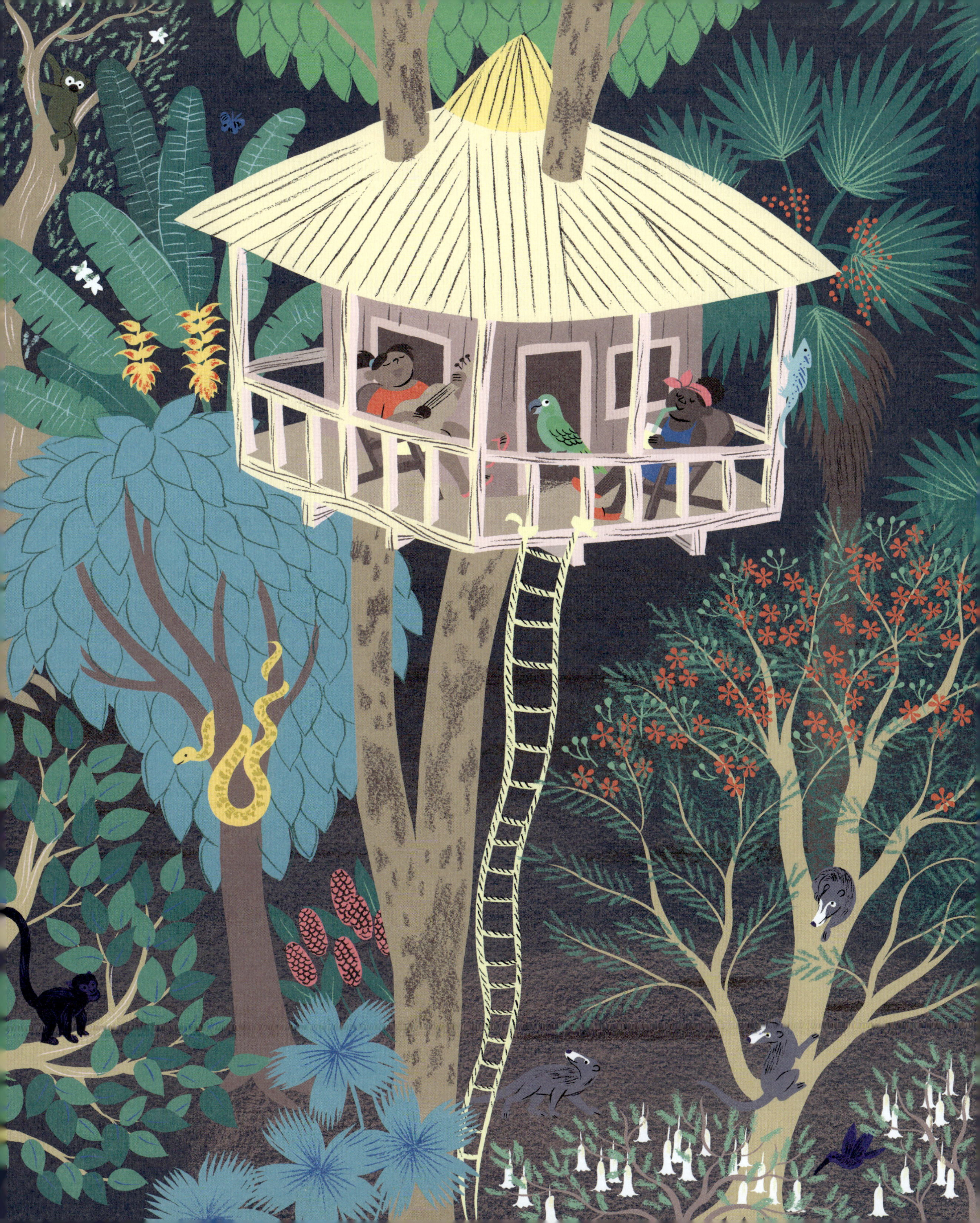

I took a boat to get to Antonio's home. It is a type of cabin called a trabucco. With long poles sticking out of it, that look a bit like arms, the trabucco looks like a big bug ready to fly off. The nets that hang off the arms allow Antonio to fish straight from his kitchen without ever getting wet. On days when he does want to get in the water, the cabin's huge pier is perfect to dive from. With his fins and diving mask on, Antonio feels like a fish himself. His neighbour, the octopus, lives in an old treasure chest and shakes his tentacles as if to say hello. While Antonio catches fish for our dinner, I watch the seagulls floating on the water.

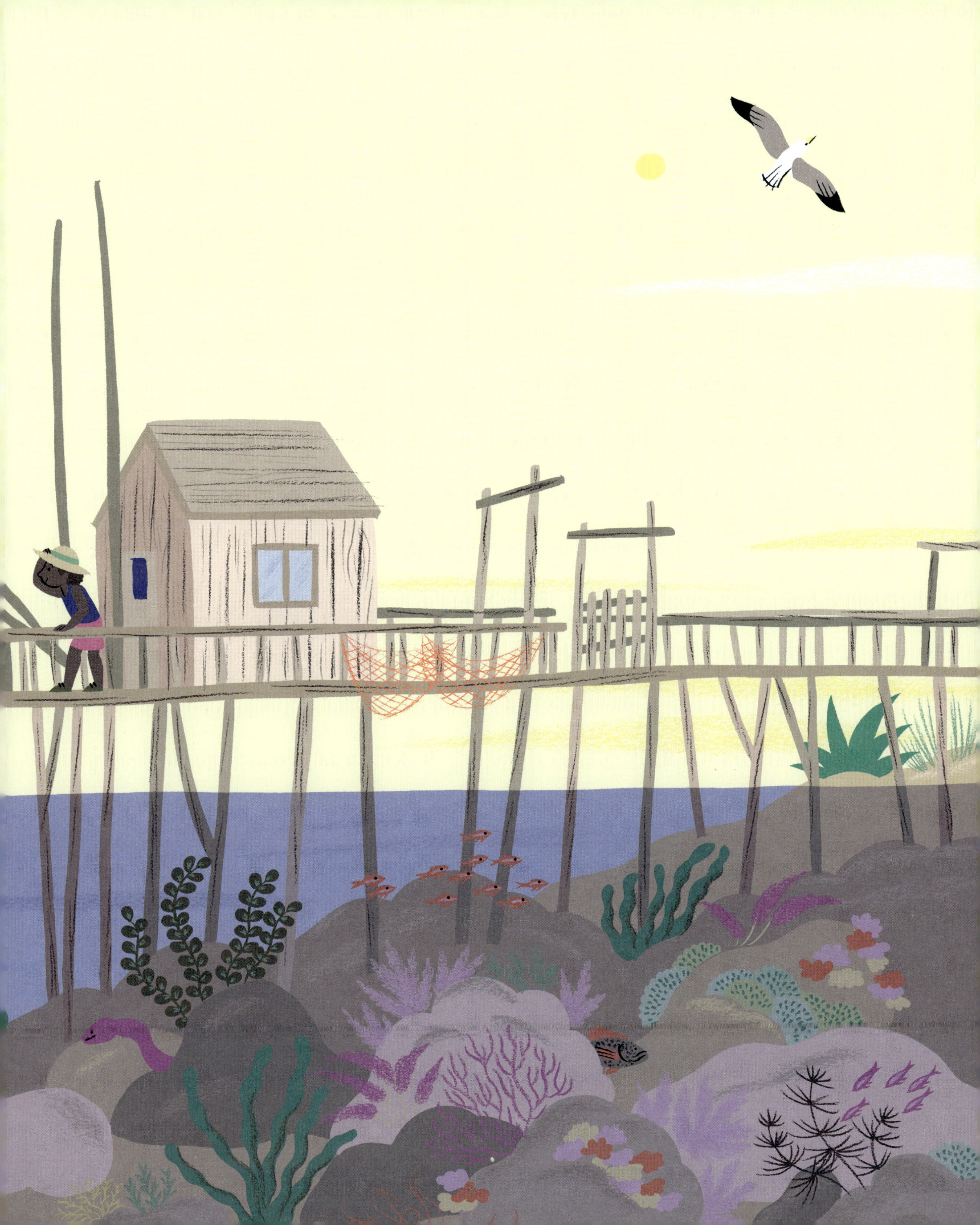

My next visit is to Victor, whose cabin was built by his grandfather. It is so old that it has no running water. If we want to wash up or have a drink, we have to get water from the hidden spring. On our daily trips there, Victor and I pass furry rodents called marmots, who whistle at us. The sheep pay them no attention, as they are more interested in Victor's dogs, Lucky and Luna, who watch over the flock. At night, the sky is full of bright stars – if we're lucky we can spot the two bear constellations in the Milky Way. Victor and I count sheep and stars until we fall fast asleep.

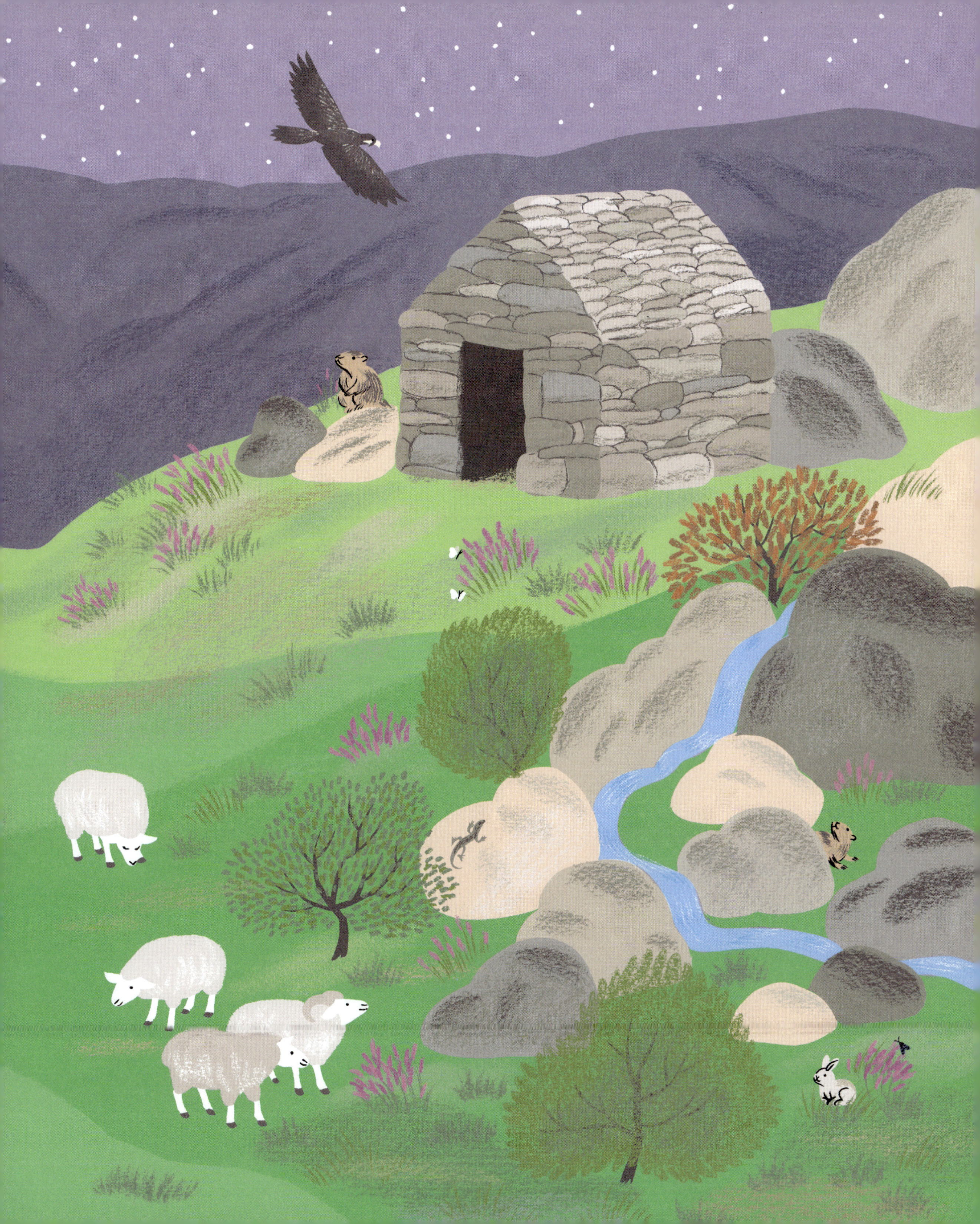

Sakari's cabin was built without using a hammer and nails. It's an igloo, made from blocks of ice cut with a saw so they fit together perfectly. The entrance to the igloo is low to the ground so we have to bend down to get inside – it's a good thing that neither Sakari nor I are very tall! When we go outside to play or ice-fish, we always wear our warm jackets to keep out the biting cold. But when we're inside, the small, low entrance keeps out both the cold weather and the naughty seals. Sakari's little husky dogs like to think they are big, bad wolves that can scare the seals away. They also like to bark at us and pull us along the snow on their sledge.

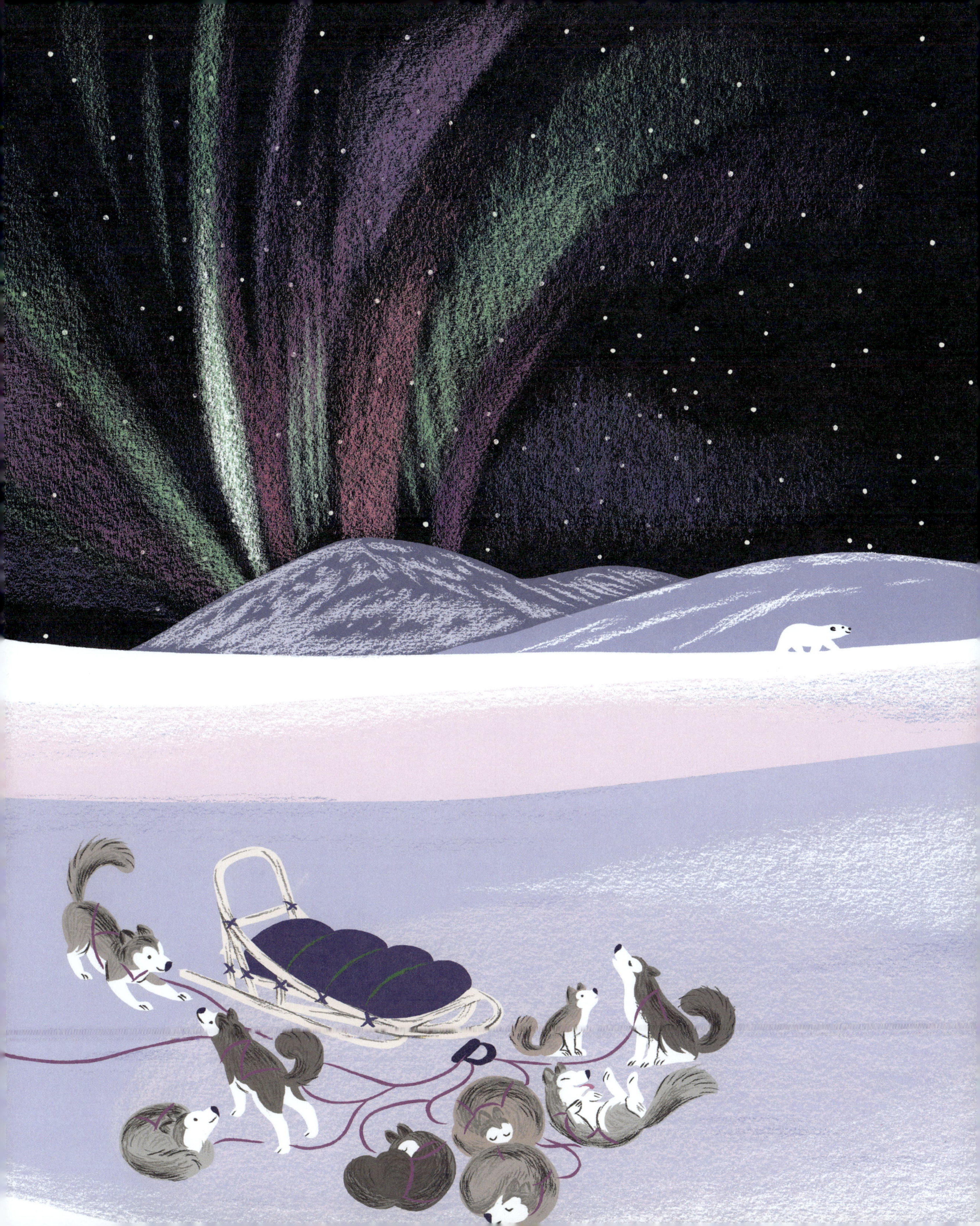

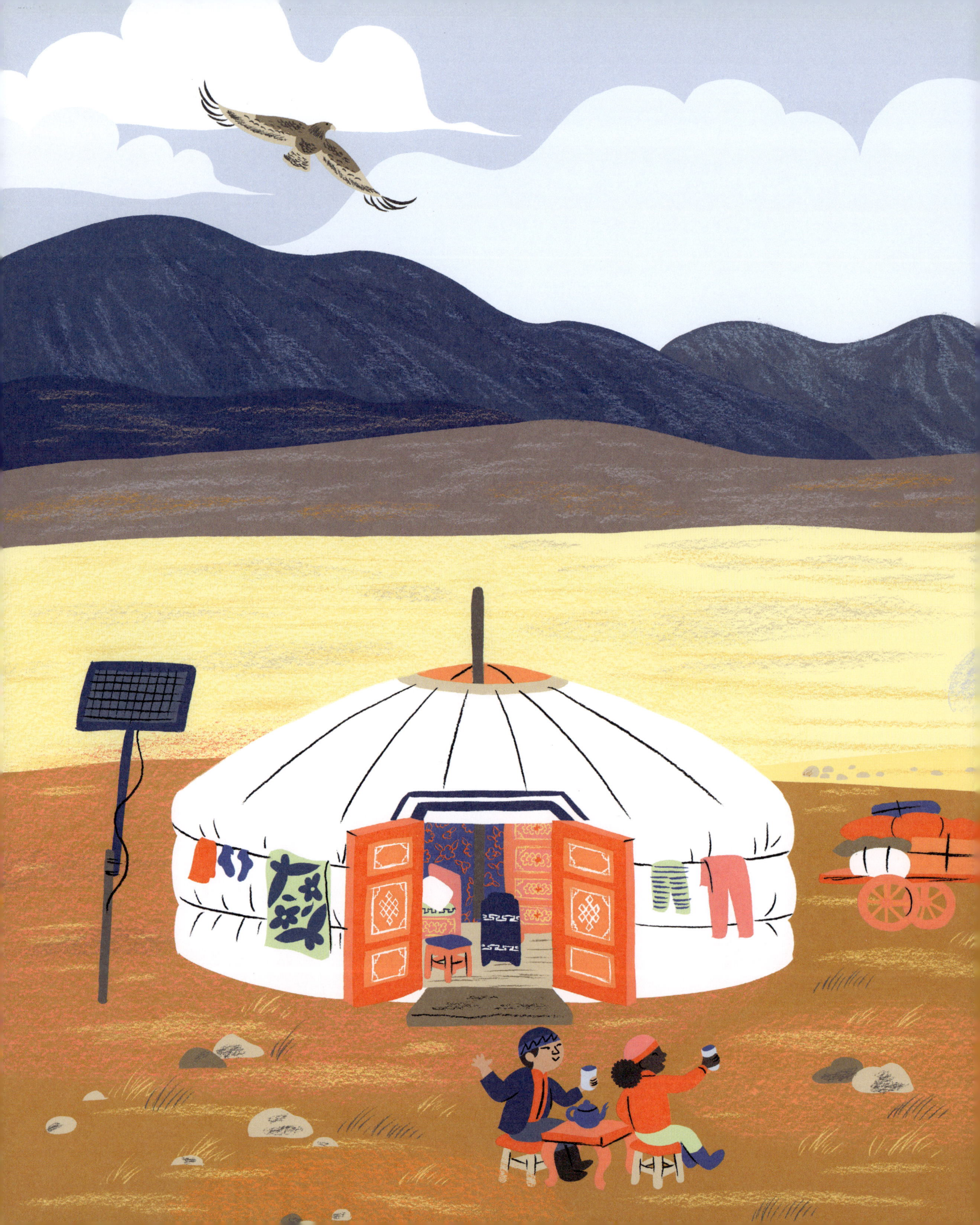

It took me a while to find my friend Gantulga's cabin. This is because it is a yurt that can be built and taken apart in an instant, to be packed up and re-built somewhere else. The door in a yurt traditionally faces south. This means that when the sun shines through the hole in the roof, Gantulga can tell the time from where the light falls. The insides of the yurt are beautiful and colourful, with a bright blue cabinet, candy-pink bed, and huge, red doors. Outside, horse riders race each other on tiny horses, and Gantulga and I cheer them on while enjoying a salty milk tea.

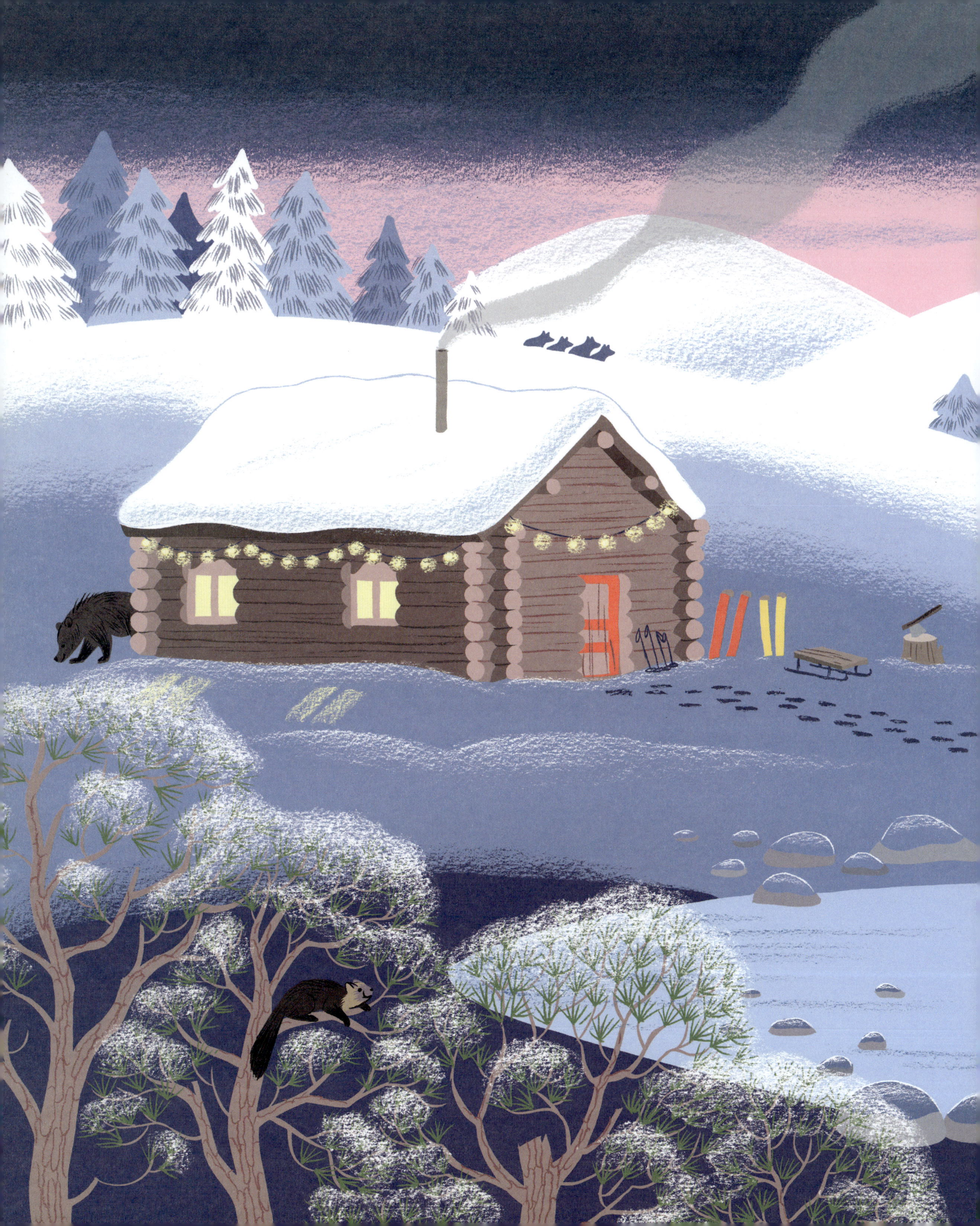

Aliocha's cabin is an izba, a type of log cabin. It's made of pine tree logs stacked on top of one another. Inside, there is a wood-burning stove that keeps us toasty warm, and we watch as the smoke escapes through the big pipe on the roof. During my stay, we take the sledge out over the snow to carry back bundles of firewood from the forest to make a bonfire. A little silver fox hears us singing and laughing and sneaks up to join us by the fire. Aliocha doesn't mind unexpected guests, so we share our fireside songs with the fox until long after sunset.

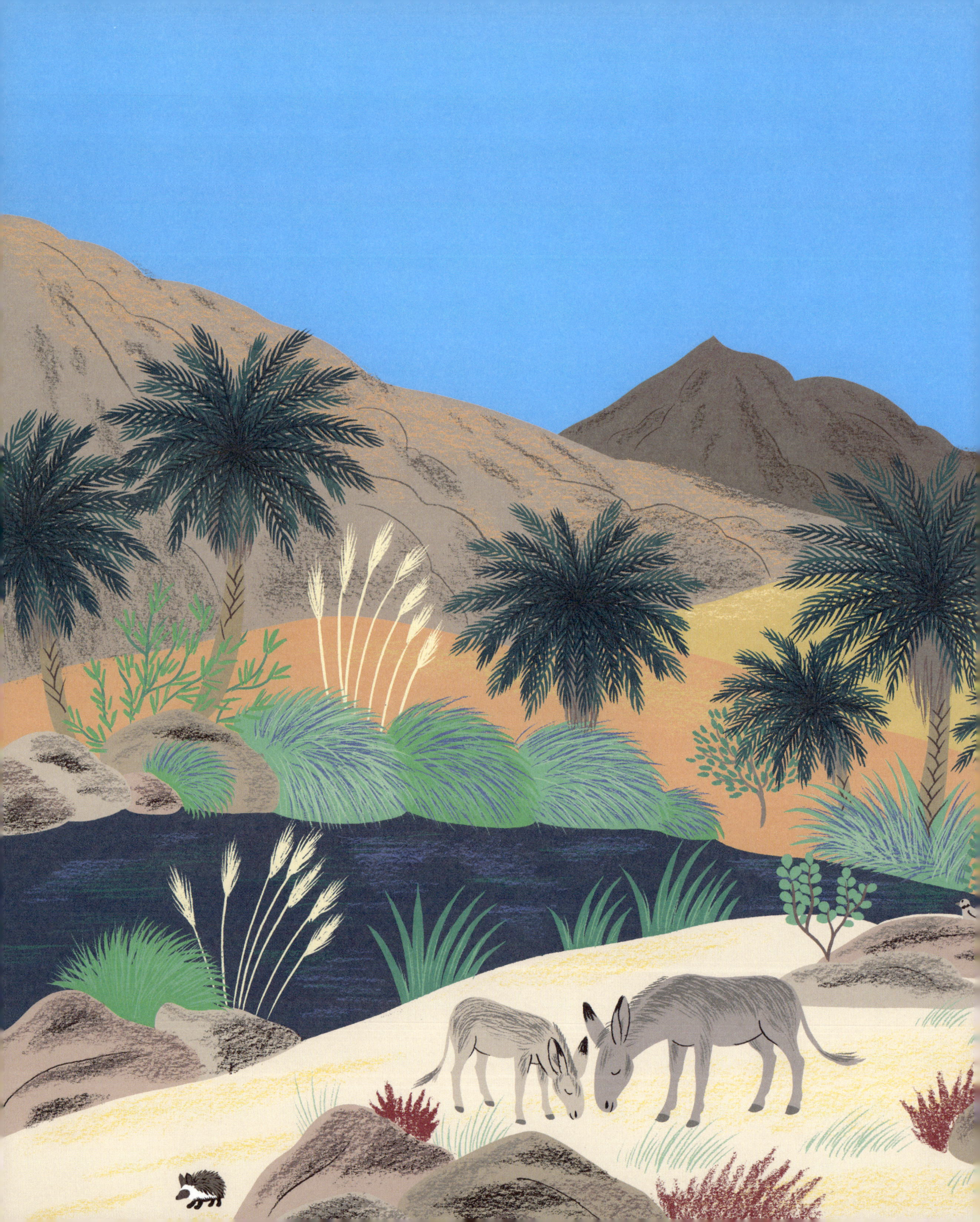

Aksil's cabin is a reed hut called a zeriba. Covered with dried palm leaves and reeds, it can protect us from the fiercest storms and from the burning desert heat. It's also near a pool of cool water where all the animals come to drink. This makes it the ideal summer home, which is why Aksil returns every summer. No one moves around in the heat of the day: Aksil and I challenge each other with riddles, the fennec foxes sleep soundly in the shade, and the camels that carried us here take a well-earned rest.

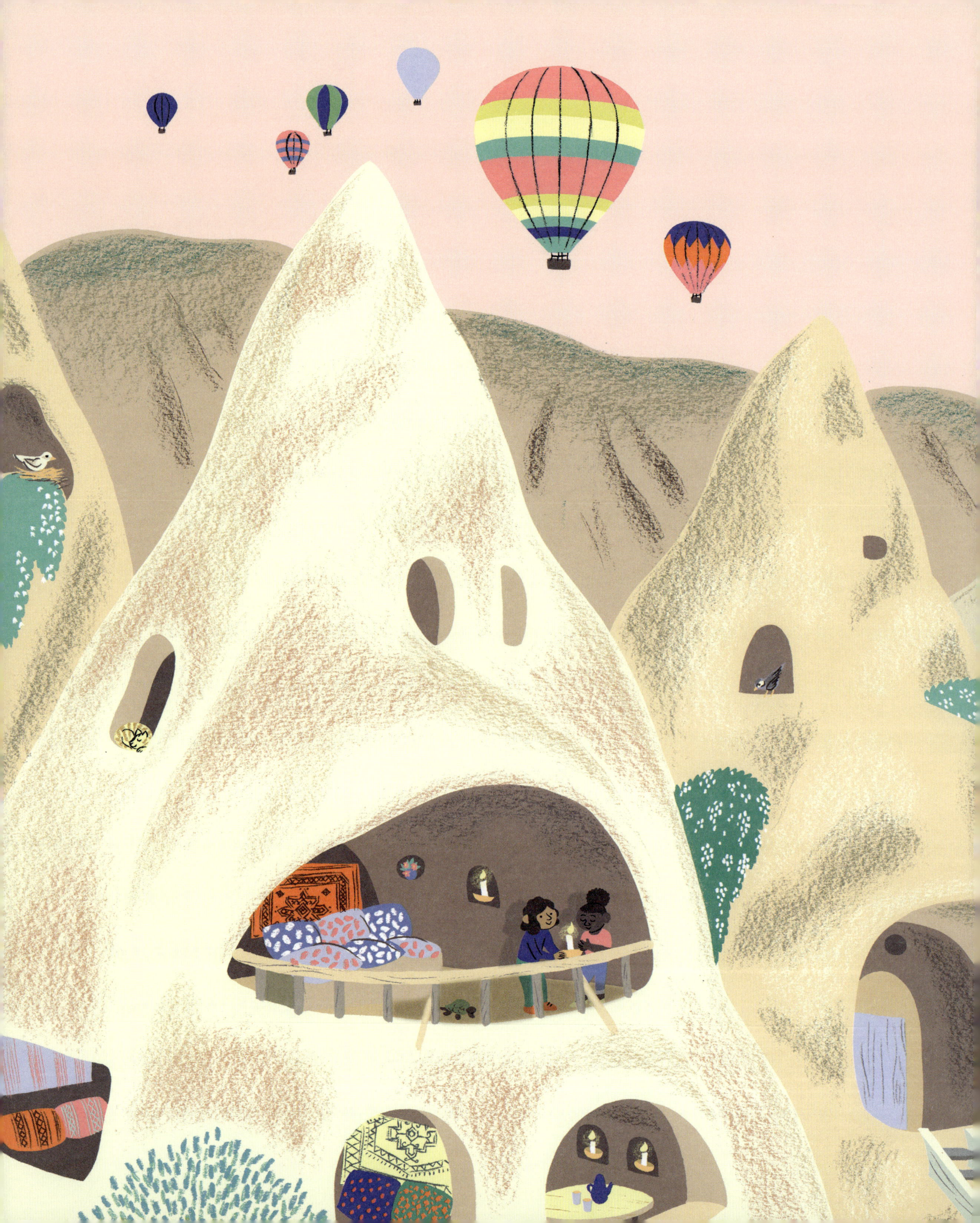

Esra's cabin is a home carved out of rock, surrounded by hills. It almost looks like he lives on the moon! Colourful hot air balloons soar in the sky above the cabin, with passengers enjoying the scenery. The cabin's stone interior means that the temperature inside is always ideal: cool in the summer and cosy in the winter. There is no electricity for light, so when the Sun goes down, Esra and I burn candles. The candlelight makes our shadows stretch up the walls as we tell each other ghost stories late into the night.

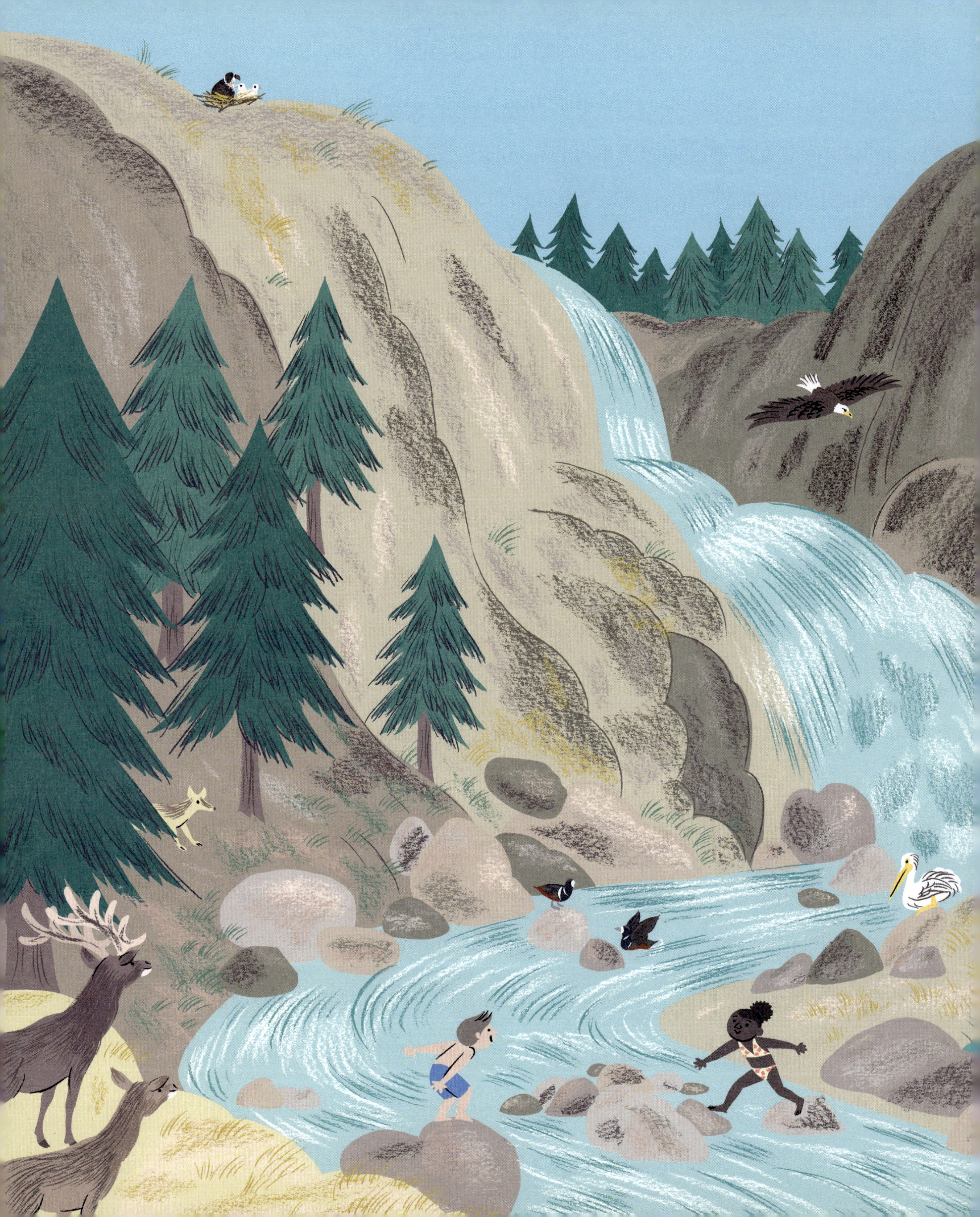

Max's cabin is made for adventures. Half cabin, half caravan, you can move this wooden home anywhere – near a volcano, close to the ocean, or in a meadow or forest. The cabin may be small, but it gives us everything we could need: a place to wash, a place to eat, and a place to sleep. It's incredible that the tiny solar panel on the roof can make enough energy to power Max's entire home! Max and I decide to park up by an icy mountain stream. While we take a dip in the cold water, bald eagles fly over us, going to and from their nest.

Ahuura's cabin faces the ocean. I arrive there from the beach by climbing up the blue and white stairs. The parrotfish and the grinning sharks cheer me on as Ahuura teaches me to surf. After a day of being out in the Sun, we take a rest in the shade of the frangipani trees surrounding the cabin. I see Ahurra's neighbour, Gavin the gecko, sitting in the tree as I pack my bag. It's nearly time for me to go home and build my own dream cabin. But which one was the best?

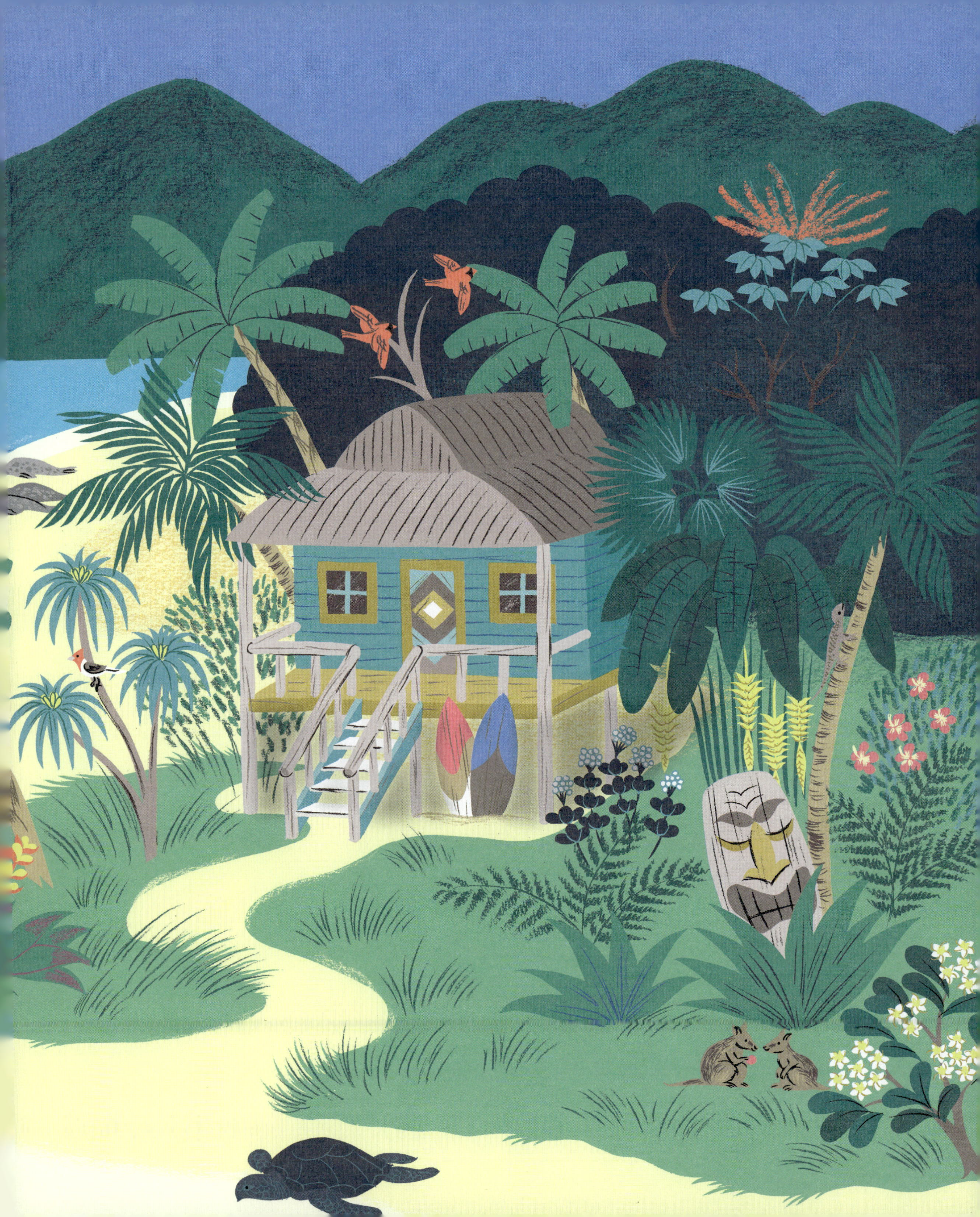

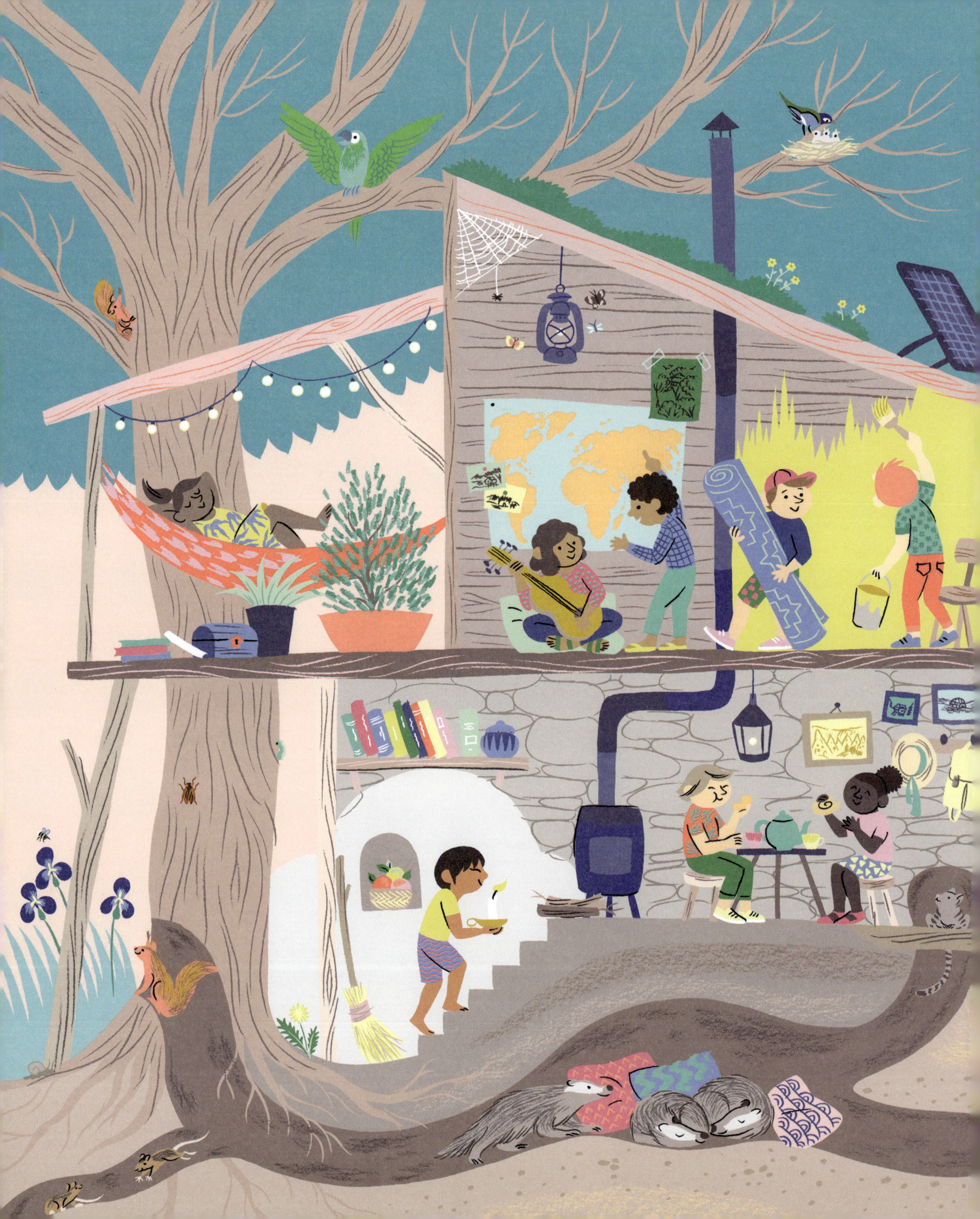

I loved visiting all my friends and seeing their different homes. It made me realize that my perfect cabin doesn't have to be one thing. It can have walls made of old stone or planks of pine, a roof of reeds or canvas, and you can reach it by a rope ladder or straight from the sea. It can be built on ice or sand, and it can have shiny solar panels and a cosy fireplace all at once. But what's most important is that in my dream cabin, there is lots of space for all my friends to visit me.

My search for the perfect cabin took me to different parts of the world. From an igloo in Canada to a zeriba in Algeria, I saw them all and learned a lot. Here are some more facts that I learned while I was visiting my friends.

Costa Rica is a small country but it has more than 900 types of birds, such as toucans, macaws, and Anna's mint-coloured parrot.

resplendent quetzal

cardamom buns

macaw

These tasty treats are very common in **Sweden** and are known as semla.

Erik's neighbour, the elk, is actually the national animal of **Sweden**.

elk

toucans

The constellations (patterns of stars) that can be seen from Victor's cabin in **France** are said to be of a mother bear or "The Great Bear" and her son "The Little Bear".

The Great Bear

The Little Bear

Fishing is a big tradition in Apulia, **Italy**, but there is often stormy weather. Trabuccos help people, like Antonio, fish easily without having to go out on the rough water.

The Northern Lights can't be seen from many places in the world, but Sakari can spot them in **Canada**. They show up when it is dark and fill the sky with ripples of colour.

Northern Lights

trabucco

yak

In **Mongolia**, yaks not only produce the milk for the tea, but they also carry and transport packed up yurts.

silver fox

The silver foxes in **Siberia** have amazingly thick fur that even covers the bottom of their feet!

salty milk tea

This hot drink is made up of water, milk, tea leaves and salt, and is served with nearly every meal in **Mongolia**!

cave homes

People have been making homes out of the caves in **Turkey** since 300 CE. In fact, entire cities have come from these rocks!

aleshu clothing

In **Algeria** in North Africa, people wear light, indigo clothes called aleshu to help them keep cool in the heat.

bald eagle

The bald eagle that Max and Lucile spotted is the national bird of the **USA**.

raised housing

Raised cabins like Ahuura's are common in Hawaii, **USA**, as it protects homes from flooding.

About the author

Emmanuelle Mardesson was born in Orléans, France, in 1977. She studied law and cinema before pursuing a career as an author. As well as writing *My Perfect Cabin*, Mardesson's other works include *The City of Animals* and *Animal Duos*, both with illustrator Sarah Loulendo.

About the illustrator

Sarah Loulendo was born in Rouen, France, in 1983. She studied fashion design at the Duperré School of Applied Arts, then at the Decorative Arts in Paris. Taking her diplomas with her, she left France to work as a stylist and graphic designer in Barcelona, Spain, and then Stockholm, Sweden. Returning to Paris in 2009, she became a textile graphic designer in the children's fashion sector. Currently she is working as a freelance illustrator, pursuing her passion of print creation.

Acknowledgements Dorling Kindersley would like to thank: Roohi Sehgal, Kritika Gupta, and Satu Fox for editorial support; Romi Chakraborty and Monica Saigal for managerial support; Issy Walsh for jacket co-ordination; and Marie Lecouturier and Yannick Hansen for translation assistance.

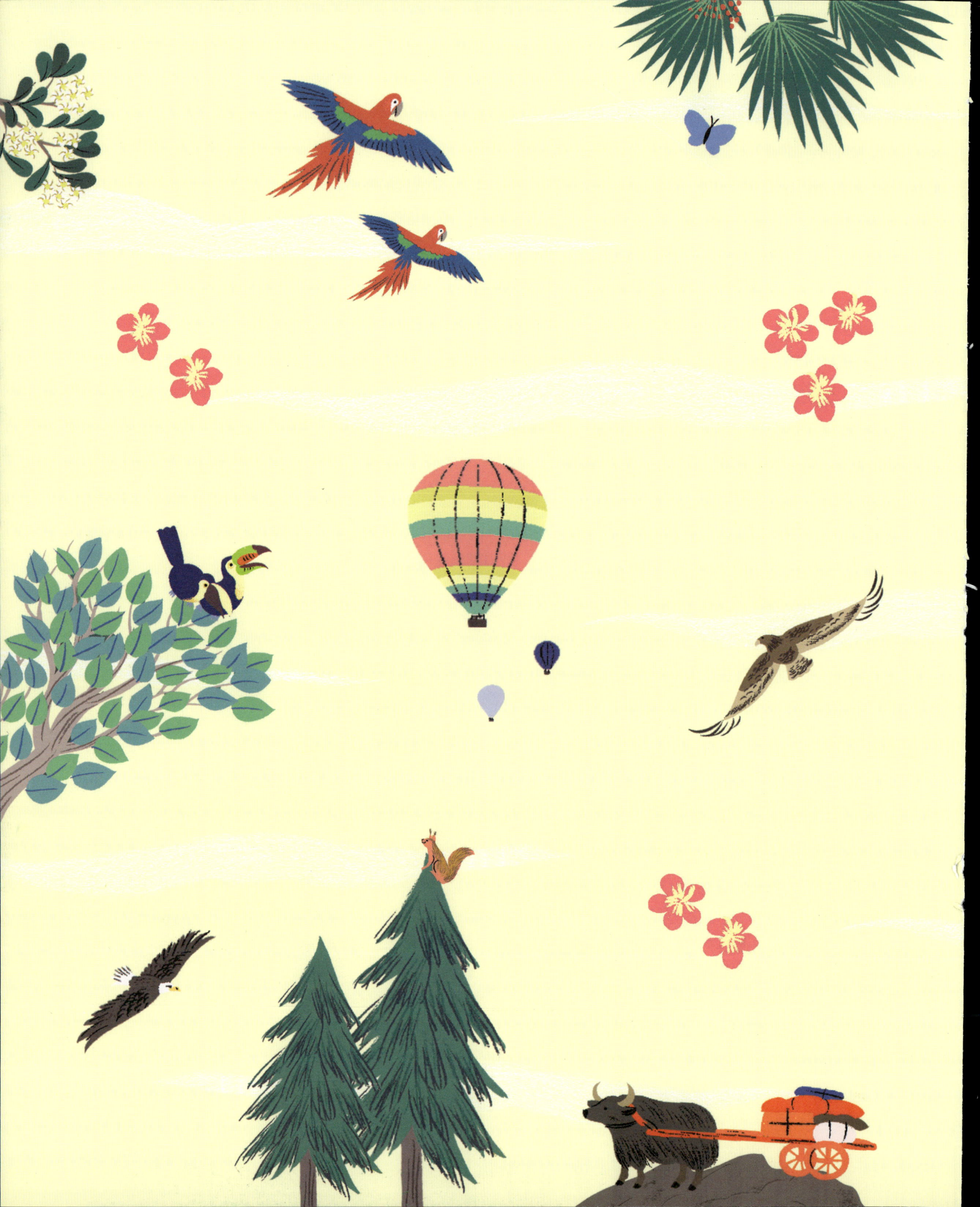